# MONEY

*The Beginner's Guide to Successfully Make Money Online*

# TABLE OF CONTENTS

Introduction ................................................................. 5

Selling on Amazon ..................................................... 9

Affiliate Marketing ................................................... 16

Investing .................................................................. 28

Life Coaching .......................................................... 36

YouTube Partnership ............................................... 43

Precautions .............................................................. 49

Conclusion ............................................................... 56

© Copyright 2017 by _____ - All rights reserved.

The following eBook is reproduced below with the goal of providing information that is as accurate and as reliable as possible. Regardless, purchasing this eBook can be seen as consent to the fact that both the publisher and the author of this book are in no way experts on the topics discussed within, and that any recommendations or suggestions made herein are for entertainment purposes only. Professionals should be consulted as needed before undertaking any of the action endorsed herein.

This declaration is deemed fair and valid by both the American Bar Association and the Committee of Publishers Association and is legally binding throughout the United States.

Furthermore, the transmission, duplication or reproduction of any of the following work, including precise information, will be considered an illegal act, irrespective whether it is done electronically or in print. The legality extends to creating a secondary or tertiary copy of the work or a recorded copy and is only allowed with an express written consent of the Publisher. All additional rights are reserved.

The information in the following pages is broadly considered to be a truthful and accurate account of facts, and as such any inattention, use or misuse of the information in question by the reader will render any resulting actions solely under their purview. There are no scenarios in which the publisher or the original author of this work can be in any fashion deemed liable for any hardship or damages that may befall them after undertaking information described herein.

Additionally, the information found on the following pages is intended for informational purposes only and should thus be considered, universal. As befitting its nature, the information presented is without assurance regarding its continued validity or interim quality. Trademarks that mentioned are done without written consent and can in no way be considered an endorsement from the trademark holder.

# INTRODUCTION

Congratulations on downloading your personal copy of *Money: The Beginner's Guide to Successfully Make Money Online*. Thank you for doing so.

The following chapters will discuss some of the many ways that you can earn money online. With the way technology has weaved its way into every fiber of society, it has caused a huge change in how we work, live, and entertain ourselves. Because of the disruptive nature of the internet, the rate at which things have changed has increased exponentially in the past few years.

Even with this change and an almost instant access to the population around the world through things like social media and google, there are lots of people that are still confused by how they can use this internet technology to make money.

The reason there is such a problem is that it's not easy making money online. With all the competition and people vying for attention, going through all this and finding trustworthy sources to gain a respectable income through the internet has become more challenging.

People tend to run into Internet Marketers who typically have poor intentions of getting your money instead of helping you. This isn't something new though. People have long been falling for affiliate marketing scams, network marketing, and pyramid schemes since before the internet became mainstream.

So where do we look to find ways to make legitimate money online? We're not just talking about making passive income, but to create active income through internet conveniences that will our debts, and empower users to invest and save.

It's not going to be easy. If somebody tells you otherwise, then they aren't being completely truthful. It will take a lot of effort before you start to see the profits start pouring in really. However, this book is going to give you step-by-step guides to five different ways to make money online. The important thing is to pick what you will want to spend time doing. They all will take some planning and work, and none of them you can just jump into.

## Will You Benefit from Reading the Book?

Online money-making isn't for everybody, so before we dive into this, you need to make sure that this will be something that you can do. Let's look at what skills and tools you will need in order to be successful.

- Self-motivation: This is probably the most important trait for people who work at home online. Working alone has perks, but you have to make sure you don't need external motivation.

- Good communication: Your communication will be through email and phone since you work alone, so you need to be able to express yourself clearly. This not only means being able to convey your message clearly but also have good English and grammar skills.

- Resourceful: When you work alone, you're the only person you can turn to. You will have to solve your problems without the help of colleagues.

- Tech-savvy: You're not going to have IT to help fix your computer when things mess up. You will need to know the basics of how to troubleshoot tech problems.

- Confidence: You need to be confident in your skills if you plan on being successful working on your own. If you don't believe in yourself and your skills, then you probably won't fare well.

- Reliable and fast internet

- Properly functioning computer

- Time zone converter if you plan on traveling while working

- Skype or Google+ Hangouts if your work will require you to contact people or clients.

- Computer stand and a laptop bag. Make sure that you are comfortable and ensure you can take your computer with you wherever you go.

There are plenty of books on this subject on the market, thanks again for choosing this one! Every effort was made to ensure it is full of as much useful information as possible. Please enjoy!

# SELLING ON AMAZON

The first online money-making option is by selling on Amazon. This is probably one of the most popular options next to using affiliate marketing through a blog or website. Let's look at how to get started.

**Part One: Before Registering**

*Step One: Decide on what you are going to sell.*

All sellers have access to more than 20 product categories, and professionals have access to at least ten more. Some products will require approval before you can sell them, while others do not.

Both professionals and individuals can list in these categories unless specified otherwise. You may have to meet certain requirements for certain products.

- Wine – this requires approval
- Watches – this requires approval
- Video games and consoles
- Video, Blu-Ray, and DVD – this requires approval
- Toys and games

- Tools and home improvement
- Sports collectibles – this requires approval
- Sports
- Computer games and software
- Sunglasses, shoes, and handbags – this requires approval
- Professional services – this requires approval
- Personal computers
- Outdoors
- Office Products
- Musical instruments
- Music
- Travel accessories and luggage – this requires approval
- Jewelry – this requires approval
- Scientific and Industrial
- Garden and home
- Advertising and historical collectibles – this requires approval
- Personal care and health

- Handmade
- Grocery – this requires approval
- Find are – this requires approval
- Consumer electronics
- Electronic accessories
- Entertainment Collectibles – this requires approval
- Book Collectibles
- Collectible coins – this requires approval
- Accessories and clothing – this requires approval
- Cell phones
- Photo and camera
- B2B products
- Books
- Beauty
- Baby products
- Powersports and Automotive – this requires approval
- Amazon Kindle
- Amazon device accessories

If you're just starting out, it's best to private label a product. This means that you look for a product that's already on Amazon that is profitable, and place your own packaging on it. You can check out [Amazon's Bestsellers](#) list to figure out what you should sell.

*Step Two: Pick a supplier*

After you know what you want to sell, you will need to find a supplier where you can use private label a product. This is especially helpful for people who are going to use the FBA program (fulfilled by Amazon). You can find products through Google for US suppliers, or you can use websites like Alibaba. You should also ask for samples so that you know it's good quality and worth selling. If you pick sites like Alibaba, you will be paying less for items than if you pick a US supplier, but there are some things you should pick a US supplier for.

Since you are private labeling, you will also want to come up with product labeling so that people know that it's yours.

*Step Three: Pick your selling plan*

Amazon offers two selling plans which give you the ability to be able to sell just one item or thousands of items. The professional plan gives you the chance to sell as many products as you want for a monthly fee of $39.99. The individual plan doesn't require a monthly fee but charges

$0.99 for each item you sell. With both plans, there are other selling fees when an item is sold.

If you choose to have Amazon fulfill orders for you, you will also be charged order fulfillment fees, as well as, optional services and storage fees.

Referral fees are also charged for every item that is sold. Each category has different referral fee percentages that range from six percent to 45 percent. For any media item that you sell, Amazon will charge a variable closing fee. This closing fee is $1.80.

*Step Four: Register*

Once you have figured out what to sell, and which plan works for you, as well as if you are going to go the fulfilled by Amazon route, you can register and start listing your items.

**Part Two: After Registering**

*Step Five: List*

Depending on which plan you have, you can list an item one at a time, or you can list large batches making use of their bulk tools.

You have two options of listing items: First, is through products that have already been listed on Amazon.com. All you do is tell how many of a certain product you have to sell, what the condition is, and the shipping options. Second, is to list something that isn't already on Amazon.com. First, you will have to find the items UPC/EAN and SKU. Then you can list its attributes like a title and description.

*Step Six: Selling*

After you have listed your items, customers can now see them on Amazon. The important thing is to make sure that customers see that your offer is complete and accurate, including the best product photos.

*Step Seven: Ship*

You will be notified when a customer has placed an order for your product. If you use FBA, then Amazon will do everything for you. You can also handle the shipping process by yourself.

*Step Eight: Get Paid*

Amazon will deposit payments into your bank at regular times and will notify you when they are getting ready to send you a payment.

**Expectations**

Know what to expect when it comes to income is helpful before you begin selling. The problem is, this is subjective to the person and the product. But I'll try to give you an idea of what's possible.

## MONEY

One woman was able to earn a base profit of $10,000 during the first five months of selling. She earned $42,000 during your second year by selling toys and using FBA. One man was able to earn almost $400 in profits in his first month using FBA, and then $1,784 during his second month.

This will all depend on what you are selling, how much inventory you have to start with, and if you choose to handle your supply on your own or use FBA.

# AFFILIATE MARKETING

The second money-making online option is affiliate marketing. Who in their right mind would say no to making passive income?

In order to be able to make passive income, you will have put in some time. To succeed with affiliate marketing, there are several steps you have to take before you see that first profit. These steps are not quite so passive. If you are determined to make it happen and are willing to put in the effort and time, you are already set up for success.

The work that you are willing to put in is what will help you to get your first sale. There's nothing like your very first sale to help you get motivated and ensure that you continue with your work.

What needs to happen to get you started? There are five steps to help you make your first affiliate commission. If you can follow these steps, you will be on the right path to earning your first commission.

**Step One: Find a niche**

Before you start building a site, you have to decide what niche you will be targeting.

If you haven't got a clue about the site that you want to make, or if you are unsure of your target market, you aren't going to be able to make a good site.

If you know what it's going to be, great! This is the most difficult step. If you can't quite figure out what you want your niche to be about, then try asking yourself some of these questions:

- *What things are you most passionate about?*

It makes it easier to do something. If you have a passion for something, you already know something about it, so that's a plus.

- *Are you able to make money in the niche that you want?*

It's great to follow your passion, but you sometimes need to think about the money that can be made and getting in on a profitable niche is sometimes better. It could be a niche that you don't know much about, but with the money you could make, you would be willing to learn, right?

- *What topic can I write 100 blogs about?*

No matter the topic you pick, you need to make sure that there is enough depth to it so that you can write a lot of content. You need this in order to build an authoritative site, to have better SEO, and for the person who will use the information. If you are unable to research enough content about your niche, then your readers aren't going to take you seriously, and you won't be able to convince others to make a purchase from you.

- *Is there a place for another affiliate in this niche?*

You can find lots of profitable niches that are popular within affiliate markets. Before jumping in with both feet, so make sure that there is a place for you. Are you going to be able to compete with others as well as make money? If the answer is no, keep looking.

- *Is there any interest or demand for you niche?*

You niche may bring in people to read about it, but are these people going to be willing to buy products as well? Your niche won't make money if there isn't any interest in the product.

- *Are you about to find programs within your niche?*

This is extremely important. You may have an idea that you know a lot about, but is there room for another affiliate program within this niche? No room equals no sales. Look at something else.

**Step Two: Research Affiliate Programs**

After you have decided upon your niche, you will have to figure out the products and programs that you want to promote. You may have done some research while looking for a niche. Now just dig a bit deeper.

Choosing a program does take time and work, but you can't be afraid to spend a lot of time on this since it will be your source of income. If you can choose the right program, it is going to be well worth the time.

Keep these points in mind when looking for an affiliate program:

- *What merchants are going to use the affiliate network?*

You have to make sure that there will be other sellers using the network because this will help you see if you will be successful with this type of program.

- *How much of a profit are you looking to make on these products?*

You should only pick programs that will give you a return and are profitable. Here are some tips:

1. For actual products, look for one that has commissions over $40.

2. For cost-per-action programs, the commissions need to be over one dollar, and products don't need to be restrictive in how you are able to promote them.

3. If using ClickBank, products need to have at least a 50 percent commission preferably 60 percent and must be in demand.

- *Do you feel comfortable being associated with these products and services?*

The services and products that you are promoting must be good quality and relevant. You need to believe in them and know all there is to know about them since this is critical to you making a sales pitch to your readers. You need to create some trust with your audience, so you need to make sure the services and products are trustworthy.

- *Does the program provide any support?*

See if your program offers any customer support after you sign up. Research if at all possible, talk to other sellers that use the program and get their opinions. Are there people you can talk to by phone or Skype? Are you going to have to wait up to 72 hours to get a response through email? You are going to need support at some point. You need to know who and how to get in touch with someone.

**Step Three: Build a site**

The first two steps are about researching and knowing what is profitable and possible. Not, put your research in action.

If you do not already have a website, then that will need to be the next thing you do. Making a website isn't as labor-intensive or complicated at it use to be.

WordPress is a great way to go if you are new at building sites. This site is easy to use and don't require any technical knowledge to get your site up and running. Coding skills can come in handy, but you aren't going to need it.

Here are some steps to follow to get your site going:

- *Buy a domain*

This is your website address. This is the first thing that you have to figure out when you start to make your site. Because the internet has so many sites, the name you want might already be taken. You need to have several options in mind. There are lots of different places you can go to purchase a domain name like NameCheap, GoDaddy, and Affilorama Domain.

- *Buy and set up your hosting*

Your domain is like an actual house where your site is going to live. It's a little piece of internet real estate. This is where your files are going to live. Hosting is cost efficient now, so you shouldn't scrimp on cost. Locate a reputable and reliable provider since your business is going to depend on it

- *Install WordPress*

Once you have your hosting ready, you have to install CMS for the site. WordPress is easy for beginners. Many providers will give you a one-click install. This means it's only going to take a couple of minutes to install it.

- *Install your theme*

Your WordPress theme gives you all the styling your site is going to need. This is what your audience is going to see when they click on your site. There are thousands to choose from, and it might seem impossible. Go with something simple that is easily customizable. You can change it up later.

The AffiloTheme is a good option. You can customize it and it's perfect for affiliate marketers. You are able to use it to bypass most of what other marketers will experience.

- *Create content*

When your site is ready, now you need to create content. The content needs to be related to your niche and it has to be interesting and engaging so that your readers will continue to come back. Make sure the content is search engine friendly, which means that the website is easily found through search engines.

## Step Four: Produce Excellent Content

You've joined an affiliate program, and your site is ready to go, now you are ready to start the time-consuming part, but the most rewarding. That is producing content.

This is where you have to start adding content.

The purpose of your website is to make you look like an authority within your niche. The easiest way to do this is to produce the best content.

Your content should be made up with:

- Product reviews: You can base your site on writing product and service reviews. This is normal and if you can do it well, can be extremely useful in making affiliate income.

- Blog posts that address issues, questions, or problems that are relevant to your niche: Creating content is an effective and useful way to add more content to your site. When making blog posts, do some keyword research to find what your audience is searching for and interested in online. Research competitors, social media, and forums to narrow down topics for your site.

- Evergreen content: If your site can possibly end up being a source of information that doesn't age and stays relevant, then you have a chance of making a website called evergreen content. You have to do extensive research on keywords before you plan your content. Your site might benefit a lot from the use of the right keywords.

- Informational products: Giving away free informational products like a mini course, an email series or an e-book is a great tactic to use. Readers have to give up email addresses to get these products. You can use them to sell to other email marketers. All informational products could generate interest in the products you are selling. If the product is popular and brings a lot of traffic, you can monetize traffic other ways.

## Step Five: Promote Affiliate Offers

This is what you have been wanting to learn about. When you have shown that you have something to offer that can bring value to your niche, you can now start to add value by doing promotions that your audience will find useful.

You can do promotions in different ways. It depends on the type of site and what you are selling. Here are some ideas:

- Product reviews: Provide your honest opinions. This is where you build trust so that they know they can take your opinion seriously. Don't only state what the positives are and sugar coat the bad. Honest opinions are values.

- Banner ads: Add banners to your website to promote products. Most of the time, the programs will give you their own banner when you pick offers. You just need to insert their banner on your page.

- In-test content links: These are links to services and products that if a reader clicks through and buys something that you will get a commission on. You will blend these with content on your site and are good for promoting offers in your content.

- Email promotions: You can promote offers through email. You need to have a relationship with your readers before you try to sell them something.

- Giveaways and discounts: Most programs run promotions that offer giveaways or discounts that could be attractive to your audience. If you are an affiliate of Amazon and they are having a huge sale, this is a great opportunity to promote discounts to your visitors.

You need to make sure you understand all of the conditions and terms that come along with affiliate programs. There are some that have strict rules about you promoting their products. Some may only allow you to use banners, ads, or links. Other will allow you to do paid advertisements, but won't let you use email marketing.

You will also need to add a disclaimer to your site to let your readers know that the links may promote affiliate content. This is a courtesy to your visitors and might be necessary for many programs.

Now that you've been through all these steps, the next step is just to keep doing what you have been doing. That's it.

Your work as an affiliate marketer is repeating steps four and five continuously. Building a site where it makes you a constant income takes work, and you have to sell consistently, innovate, market, promote, and create.

At first, it will feel overwhelming when you first start your site and you are working to build a reputation. When you make your first sale, it will all be worth it.

Making your first commission takes some hard work, but if you can follow all the steps, it's not going to seem that hard. Here's a quick recap.

1. Pick your niche.
2. Do research on different affiliate products and programs.
3. Make a website.
4. Come up with content.
5. Promote your products.

There is a strategy behind affiliate marketing. If you put in the work, you will start reaping the rewards

**Expectations**

The normal salary for affiliate marketers is about $5,000. This is virtually no money, but it's true since many people struggle to make money online. Even if you look at super affiliate's salaries, it is still a fairly accurate figure. You will need to learn more if you want to increase these figures.

If you became a manager of a company, you could earn from $38,000 to $60,000 a year. This is a job, but you will still be affiliate marketing. This beats $5,000. This is the normal salary for affiliate marketers. Getting around this number is hard.

# INVESTING

The third option for making money online is through investing. There are many different aspects of investing and the stock market. We're going to look at long term investments, which won't make you rich overnight, nor is it a regular stream of money. This is more for the person that wants to make some passive income, and invest some extra money they have saved up.

The tricky part of the investment is what you are going to invest in and how much you are planning on investing. You will also have to decide how long you are willing to let your money grow. So, let's look at the best investment strategy to help you invest your money the right way.

**Step One: Why are you investing?**

Investing in something while you're young is a great way to see solid returns. Social Security alone probably isn't going to give you enough retirement money for you to be comfortable. Making sure that you have long-term savings is important. An investment that gives you a higher return than a regular savings account is also a great option for short-term goals.

Investing may sound like something that a parent or boss would do, but if you look at it as a puzzle, you could see why it's kind of fun. Let's look at it in a less intimidating light.

Making a stock market investment is a DIY way to have a comfortable nest egg once you have reached retirement. There are going to be ups and downs, but when you invest at a younger age, that means you will have decades to ride the stock market out. It plays another important role in retirement because Social Security only accounts for about 38% of seniors' income.

In coming decades, the number could possibly decline. For a while now, Social Security has been paying more to retirees than they have been getting in from taxes from workers.

The program had built an up a "trust fund" of sorts in order to be ready for the retirement of baby boomers, but it is projected that the reserve may be depleted by the year 2033. They are still receiving tax money, so Social Security isn't going to go completely dry. But, they won't be able to pay the complete amount that has been promised and will only pay three-quarters.

This means that if you invest in something, then you are doing yourself a big favor because you will be supplementing your retirement plan. You will make sure that you have the extra money to go to brunch and go on vacation once you reach your golden years. So, while you wait for retirement, start investing in safe assets such as bonds to help get some extra money in the short term. This can make a big difference if you are planning on purchasing a house or something else big, in the next few years.

**Step Two: What to invest in?**

No matter the way you plan on investing for retirement, be it a 401(k) or another employer-sponsored plan, Roth or traditional IRA, or an investment through a brokerage account, you have complete control in what you choose to invest your money in. You have to research each instrument so that you know how much risk comes with it.

There are many different choices for you to invest in:

- Stocks – this means you will share ownership in a certain company. The price of stocks can fluctuate depending on the investors' evaluations of how the company performs, which include leadership changes, new products, and its financial information. Companies have stocks that the public can purchase when they want to raise money so that they can grow, an example would be if they need to pay off a debt. Stocks are also sometimes referred to as equities.

- Bonds – bonds are basically a loan to a government entity or company which has agreed to pay back your investment in a certain amount of time. While you wait, you earn interest. This is a less risky choice than a stock because you know the date as to when you will be paid, and you will know the amount of money you will earn.

- Mutual funds – this is a mixture of different investments that are managed by a company. If you invest in a mutual fund, you aren't required to pick a certain stock or security; your fund will do this for you. Some popular mutual funds are index, which will follow along with the performance of certain money market funds, and stock market index, which will invest in low-risk, short-term assets. There are many risk levels associated with mutual funds. Basically, the riskier something is, the bigger the possible return will be.

**Step Three: How to figure out your strategy?**

You should choose your strategy based on how long of a savings goal you have. If you are planning on saving for retirement that's a few decades from now, you will want to invest different instruments, then if you were trying to save for a short-term goal.

Let's say that you want to invest in a Roth IRA for your retirement, and you're not planning on touching this money for another 40 years. The stock market has a tendency to be unpredictable, with a lot of fluctuations depending on how the economy is performing. But, the good thing is you're more likely to make more money over the long-term with the stock market than if you choose less risky investment options. An example is that over the past ten years the S&P 500 stock market index has had an annual average return of around 7.87%.

But if you are trying to save up for a short-term goal, such as a down payment in the next five years or so, the riskiness of the stock market makes it likely that you will end up losing money.

Once you know how many years your investment will have to earn returns, you can look into the different investment instruments that you can invest in. If you don't plan on touching the investment for more than 20 years, then you can invest most of your money in stocks. The problem is picking specific stocks, which gets complicated, so consider going with an index fund which will mirror how the entire stock market index performs.

Index funds are the best option for a beginner investor because it gives them more diversification, or it helps to make sure you have stocks in many different industries across several geographic regions. These passively managed funds perform a lot better than funds that are actively managed.

The percentage of your investment amount that you have invested in stocks will decrease as you get closer to your savings goal. So, if you want to buy a house in just a few years, a better choice would be to place your money in a bond fund or market fund. These both will give you lower returns but are safer to have your money in for a short amount of time.

**Step Four: How much money should be invested?**

You should only invest money after you know that you are able to pay your monthly bills and you have saved up, at the very least, three months of living expenses. Then you need to look at your cash flow to see what you have extra to spare. You can invest in something as little as a couple of hundred bucks at first.

Knowing where you plan on putting your money is important, but knowing how much you are going to put into it gets confusing. Before you do anything, make sure you have all of your necessary costs covered. If you don't already have a detailed budget, then you should at least write down all of your monthly expenses: entertainment, food, bills, and loan payments. Then you need to build up some savings so that you have a little emergency fund that will cover three months' worth of your living expenses.

After you have done this, you can start thinking about investing some extra cash. It's common to hear that you should invest 10% of your yearly earnings, but this isn't a very realistic choice. Allow yourself to be guided by the minimum initial investment of the vehicle you choose.

Most brokerage accounts will require an initial investment. If you picked a Fidelity Freedom 2055 mutual fund, this is a fund that's managed and will place different investments knowing you want the money by 2055, will require you to invest $2,500 initially, and keep a balance of $2,000.

If you can't afford that much just yet, then opening a Roth IRA is a good option. This is known as a container where your money stays, if you want to invest in individual funds. There are many Roth IRAs that you can find that don't require a minimum balance.

Through this account, you can invest a couple hundred in commission-free ETFs or mutual funds. This will keep you from having to save up thousands before you can make an initial investment. There are some Roth IRA accounts that are robo-advisors which allow you invest in low-cost ETFs and have an account minimum of as little as $0.

These are all great options to supplement your 403(b), 401(k), or any other employer-sponsored retirement options. If you have these options through your employer, you can add a part of your salary during each pay period to your 401(k). Most of the time you are able to choose the mix of assets that you invest this money in, depending on how risky you want to go. Some employers will match your investments with a company fund, which is extra money that will be added to your retirement fund that you will be able to access after you have stayed with your company for a certain amount of years.

**Expectations**

With all the other online money-making options I was able to give you an average of the amount of money you could make, with this option I can't. The amount you make depends too much on how the stock market acts. It also depends on how long you keep your investment, and your initial investment amount.

The important thing is to take everything in this chapter into consideration before you make your initial investment. You need to make sure you can afford it, and that you are investing in something that will make you money over either a long or short period of time; depending on when you plan on accessing it.

# LIFE COACHING

The fourth online money-making option is becoming an online life coach. This is a profession where you will be working to help other people with their lives. This is definitely one option that you should only consider if you are drawn to helping people. Don't pick something like this just for the money, do it because you want to and you enjoy helping people.

There isn't a licensing process for this job, and anybody can call themselves a life coach. This is why if you really want to do this, you need to make sure you go to the most legitimate and credible path. You should become certified and trained by a respected training program.

**Step One: Find a Training Program**

The best place to start looking is on the ICF website so that you can locate accredited schools. You can also narrow down your options by typing in the niche that interests you the most. This could mean distances or in-person learning, the language you want, and if you can get financial aid.

Most of the programs will teach completely with distance learning, either with online learning or teleclasses. There are few that have a combination of in-person and distant, and very few of only in-person. These all work great considering that most coaches will work with their clients using Skype or a phone.

You can also use Google to find programs, but these may not be ICF accredited. If you go through a company to get hired once you are licensed, they will look to see if your program was accredited, so it's important to make sure it is.

There are 150+ ICF accredited programs. Each program will require:

- Trainers with credentials by the ICF
- Comprehensive final exam
- Six coaching sessions that are observed by an experienced coach
- Code of Ethics and Competency training
- Coach skills training – 125 hours

**Step Two: Find your niche**

Before you make your final decision on a school, you need to decide what specialty or niche you want to focus on. Instead of just being called a life or business coach, look into refining that area of coaching you want to do so you can attract specific clients.

Coaching has competition, so a good way to distinguish yourself is to demonstrate the value you have in a certain focused niche. By working in a niche, you will be able to provide your clients with more relevant information.

Most programs will have classes that focus on specific niches, that's why it helps to have your niche picked before you choose your training program. But if you don't know what your niche is at the moment, that's okay. Make sure that you pick a strong general coaching program. You can go into a specific niche later if you want.

Some niches to consider are:

- Eat disorders
- Weight loss
- Addiction
- Holistic
- Fitness
- Wellness
- Health
- Achievement
- Motivation

- Performance
- Success
- Life skills
- Stress relief
- Finances
- Organization
- Development
- Transformational
- Mediation
- Religion
- Inner peace
- Teen or college direction
- Academic
- Grief
- Eldercare
- Divorce
- Marriage
- Corporate
- Retirement

- Job search
- Life passion
- Writing
- Personal image
- Marketing
- Business

**Step Three: Financial Prep**

The cost of your program will vary depending on which school you go with. The out of pocket cost can range from $3500 to $20,000, but most will fall within the $6000 to $12,000 range.

Just because some programs are more expensive, does not mean that it is better. But, keep an eye out for schools that are very inexpensive. A program should take you several months up to a year to complete.

After training costs, you will also have to consider small business costs to start your practice. You will have to figure out if you want to be a:

- Sole proprietor
- S Corporation
- Partnership

- Corporation
- Cooperative
- Limited Liability Company

They all provide you with legal protections and have different tax obligations and fees. You will need a computer and a phone, as well as an online presence. Things like social media accounts and a blog will add to your credibility and make it easier for people to connect with you.

**Step Four: Plan Ahead**

Once you are certified, there are some things that you need to do and plan for. This includes defining your target market, coming up with a business plan, and coming up with your business name and getting URL. You should open a business bank account and come up with your coaching packages as well as an agreement.

These are only a few things that you need to consider; there are much more to make sure your business is successful. If coaching is a fit for you, you will find a way to get everything done.

You won't become rich right away, but it is rewarding if it is something that you like to do. There is also room to grow.

## Expectations

Like all of the other money-making choices, the amount you can make is subjective to your experience, your niche, and the time and effort you put into it. Most life coaches will charge by the hour, and that's a price you can set on your own, but you have to make sure you're worth it. If you are brand new at this, and only became certified, nobody is going to be willing to pay you a thousand dollars an hour. It will also depend on what niche you are in. Different niches will make you more money.

On average an executive coach can make $325 an hour, a business coach can make $235 an hour, and a general life coach can make $160 an hour. For a new life coach, no matter the niche, you can probably get by with charging $100 - $200 an hour. Veteran coaches can charge up to $600 an hour.

An average annual income for a life coach can range from $55K to $116K.

# YOUTUBE PARTNERSHIP

The last money-making option online is making money with YouTube videos. We have all seen viral videos. They come in many sizes and shapes from something crazy, someone falling down, grumpy cat, to new songs and dances. What does all this have in common? These people made a lot of money on YouTube when their video went viral.

How can you make money with YouTube? Making money on YouTube isn't easy. There are hurdles you will have to overcome. It is not a get rich quick plan. If you have a hobby or are great at a certain activity and want to help people, want to have fun, or are funny, YouTube is an option to cash in on some money by doing things you love to do. Let's find out:

**Step One: Set Up an Account**

The most obvious is setting up a YouTube account. You need to know what type of video you are going to be uploading. Then you need to enable monetization and sign up for Google Ads.

Enabling monetization just means you are agreeing to upload videos that you have the right to and you are going to play by the rules like not watching your own video many times to boost your ads. Google AdSense is how you set up payment information when you begin to make money.

**Step Two: Become a YouTube Partner**

This is easier than it used to be. You used to have over 15,000 hours of your video watched before you could become a partner. You can upload over 15 minutes of video and this helps with some projects. You can get some advanced editing tools and analytical tools.

Once you have monetization setup and Google AdSense along with your YouTube partnership, you are ready.

**Step Three: Advertisements**

You are familiar with ads when you watch videos on YouTube. There is a bottom text ad that gets displayed near the bottom of the video. The other is a clip that plays before your video. You get to choose which of these you want on your videos. It can make a large difference. It all depends on how much revenue your video can bring in or your audience.

The way it works is the most complicated thing with trying to make money with YouTube. The estimate comes to about $7.50 for 1,000 views. The only way you make money is when someone interacts with the ad.

This means if somebody skips the ad, or runs an ad blocker, you won't get paid for a view. This makes estimating the number of views a video could have extremely challenging. It will depend on if the video is in front of yours or a box on the bottom of your page. This gets determined by how many people look at your ad and how much money might be made.

There are many variables that affect the amount of money you can make. The audience will help to determine the type of ad that would work for your video. If you make short videos that are funny, you aren't going to want to include a 30-second ad before it runs. The viewer is just going to skip it. YouTube has a page that you use to see each aspect of your video from location to time of the day it will be watched and demographics.

**Step Four: Generating Money**

Let's look at how you can actually make money with YouTube. The most important thing is the videos need to be about what you are passionate about. If you aren't passionate about it, it is going to show in the video. You aren't going to have any incentive to continue to make them.

Doing normally scheduled videos at an interval that you are comfortable with would be best. If you can make regular videos, viewers will subscribe to your channel faster. Subscribing just means that they are following you. When you post new videos, they are going to see it. This is a good way to get an audience and get people to view your videos regularly.

Your videos need to be high quality and short. If you do tutorials or have other reasons for keeping your videos over six minutes, it would be better if you kept them short. If you break the video down into multiple parts, it will make the content easier to watch. This will increase the probability of it getting shared.

You need to aim for a short video that has a clear message, good editing, and clear audio. Some thought beforehand means huge dividends down the road.

**Step Five: Momentum**

Now, you need to keep your videos' momentum going. You don't get into a boat and paddle one time to get where you need to go. You must keep marketing your video. This is as simple as commenting on the comments that people have left for you. You can also comment on other's videos or share your video on Twitter or Facebook. Whatever you can do to get people watching your video will be beneficial for you.

If you join a YouTube Network, you might get more views, and get more people to your video. YouTube Network is just a group of videos. The thought behind this is if you combine many similar videos together, you are going to make more money and attract more views.

Networks might have fees along with them; they may ask to have ownership of your video or other requirements. It may not be worth joining a network with all the trouble that is behind it. Try to make your own videos and money by yourself, first. When you have gained some experience, go shopping and see what's out there, what they provide and what they ask from you.

The best videos are ones that include what you love. Figure out your unique skill and make videos in this niche. This is the best way to try making money with YouTube.

**Expectations:**

There are two main ways to make money with YouTube. The first one is becoming a YouTube Partner. This is the most popular way. You have noticed the five to ten-second ads at the beginning of most videos. That is a YouTube ad. Most everyone gets approved for this. You just need to upload original, quality videos. If your channel is found to be eligible, you will see the monetization options appear under your channel's settings.

Google show ads with your videos and you will receive a part of the revenue from advertisers. They will split the proceeds 55 to 45. If an advertiser pays $100 for an ad on your video,

Google will take $45 for giving you hosting, and you will get $55. That's pretty fair.

The second one is secondary means. When a channel becomes popular, brands will approach the creator to promote products. This could be done by a sponsored video or product placement. There are means like Amazon Affiliates, Patreon, or selling your merchandise. This happens mostly by having a large audience. You could make anywhere from $400 to $2,000 per video that is sponsored.

Most YouTubers make money from the second means than they get from AdSense. Your video also gets played on the sponsors YouTube channel.

# PRECAUTIONS

You've decided you want to be your own boss. You want to separate yourself from the herds of employees to be a self-employed master of your own domain. This can pay off in many different ways.

Each gamble you take means you have to take risks that have to be weighed against any reward that you might get. To gamble with your career without thinking about these risks is reckless. It is necessary to conduct a benefit analysis before you take the leap into being your own boss. Being your own boss sounds like a dream, but it can be a lot harsher than you think.

If you go in blindly, you are going to fail. The worst thing to do is going in unprepared. The drawback to this is too much analysis could lead to paralysis. Here are some pros and cons of becoming your own boss:

**Pros**

- **Work Your Own Hours**

The main reason most people decide to become self-employed is the desire to have better work hours. We all have wanted to get another hour of sleep some mornings. Being self-employed means that you get to decide when to start and stop your day. You can take vacations when you want, stop working early and catch a movie; it's your decision. Flexibility with work hours does have some downsides, too.

- **Work Where You Want**

Most small businesses are operated by just using a mobile phone that has an internet connection. People who own these businesses can work wherever they want to. You can work at home in bed, at the beach, in a coffee shop. This is what we call freedom. Even if you need an office, shop, or practice, you get to choose that location.

- **Tax Advantages**

There are many things that will be tax deductible for you if you bought it for your business. Anything that you buy that is related to you earning an income is a business expense that can be claimed. These expenses can be anything from office furniture, cars, business insurance, advertising expenses, literally anything that you buy that is going to improve your business. The government has introduced a tax write off that is fairly substantial so keep that in mind.

- **Control Over How Much You Make**

You won't be able to complain about how much you get paid since you are responsible for your own income. This might give you the incentive to work harder since there is a link between the effort you put in and how much you can make.

- **Choose People You Want to Work With**

When you are self-employed, you don't have to work with horrible clients or work with people who make you uncomfortable. You have the power to choose who you want to associate with.

- **You Do What You Love**

You won't be made to do things that you hate by a boss that makes you feel unappreciated. You get to do what you can do best and are passionate about. You can do what you know will use your skills.

**Cons**

- **If You Don't Work, You Don't Make Money**

You can enjoy time off but all that time is not making you any money. You will be worrying about letting your customers and clients down when you don't work. You could actually work more hours when you are self-employed that you did when employed by others.

- **Irregular Pay**

Being self-employed means your income will vary as well. There may be times when you are so busy you can't breathe and other times when you don't have anything to do. This irregular pay means that paying regular bills and loan payments might become difficult. This irregular pay makes it difficult to get a home loan, but there is a big range of low doc loans you could get.

- **Keeping Your Own Books**

Excellent bookkeeping is a necessity for any small business owner, and it could take most of your time. It can be stressful, especially if you don't know how to do it properly.

- **No Benefits, Annual Leave or Sick Pay**

There may be a time that you are going to be too sick to work, but you have to because you need the money. Being your own boss means that you don't have any company benefits like company cars, insurance, or possibly gym memberships. There won't be any annual leave either.

- **Isolation**

It gets hard for people who work totally on their own. You might miss the teamwork and not share your frustrations and victories with others. You might feel like a hermit without the sports teams, social outings, and get together that working for a company offers. You get completely engrossed in your work.

- **No 401K Payments**

You are not going to have company met 401K payments being made for you. You are going to have to become very disciplined and set money aside for retirement by yourself. It will be tempting not to put aside any money when business is slow.

Being your own boss won't be smooth sailing. You are going to have to learn to take the bad with the good and make the most with having the freedom to pursue your dreams. If it all falls apart, you won't have the regret that you weren't brave enough to try.

Here are some things to think about before jumping into being your own boss with both feet:

- **You Are Completely Responsible**

When you are your own boss, you have to do everything: networking, keeping promises, creating products, invoicing, and marketing.

This means you are responsible for everything. If something happens or goes wrong, you are going to have to put your big boy/girl pants on and own up to it and find a way to fix the situation.

If you have never held a management position, this is going to be very new to you. You must remain friendly and professional. You ARE the business.

Nobody is perfect, and you are going to make mistakes. That's fine, just prepare yourself for not having anyone else to blame. Make sure you write everything down in case there is a misunderstanding.

- **Have a Backup Plan**

Don't make a jump into self-employment without having any money available. It isn't recommended to take a leap of faith without having a financial backup plan.

Save for months leading up to the change. Try your best to have at least a five-figure fund set aside.

Having the money and knowing that you are covered, will allow you to sleep at night. You won't have to pursue extremely low paying jobs to pay your bills.

Set up a budget for just the necessities. These plans don't talk about going into debt. It isn't necessary for becoming your own boss. Work as hard as you can to get your business going while you are still working a normal, full-time job.

- **Have a Strong Network**

You are not going to get anywhere without support from friends and clients.

You have to get rid of any selfish mindsets you have.

Being your own boss doesn't mean you have to do everything by yourself. It is just the opposite.

Once you have grown your client base, you can pass along any work that you can't do to others who might need it. People will remember when you lent them a hand, and they will remember when you didn't.

- **Don't Be Afraid of Failing**

When you are your own boss, failure can be your friend since it could be your companion for some time.

There isn't one business large or small that was built in a day. They are constantly changing. This is how you need to view your business.

Each time you fail, you are going to find a new direction you need to take. You aren't being stagnant. It is showing growth.

Yes, failing gets frustrating. Don't stay in this mindset. You will begin to feel sorry for yourself and get on track with what your original plans were.

Each time you fail, find out what happened and change it. There isn't any magic for success out there. Just know that you have to fail to be able to succeed.

# CONCLUSION

Thank you for making it through to the end of *Money: The Beginner's Guide to Successfully Make Money Online*. Let's hope it was informative and able to provide you with all of the tools you need to achieve your goals.

We've covered a lot of information about making money online, and hope you have found it helpful. While the five online money-making ways are not the only ones out there, it does give you a good idea of what you have to look at. Keep everything talked about in this book in mind when you set out to make online money. Don't look over the cons just because you like the thoughts of being your own boss. If you ignore the bad, then you have a good chance of failing or making it very hard on yourself. If you take everything in this book with you as you move forward, you're sure to succeed.

Finally, if you found this book useful in any way, a review on Amazon is always appreciated!

# DESCRIPTION

Since the inception of the internet, people have been trying to make money online. Yet, there are some that still find it difficult to do so successfully. This is most likely from the fact that it's hard to find reliable people online that are actually willing to help as opposed to taking your money.

With the way technology has weaved its way into every fiber of society, it has caused a huge change in how we work, live, and entertain ourselves. Because of the disruptive nature of the internet, the rate at which things have changed has increased exponentially in the past few years.

Yet, even with this change and an almost instant access to the population around the world through things like social media and Google, there are lots of people that are still confused by how they can use this internet technology to make money.

This book is here to give you online money-making strategies to help you figure out how you want to make money online. There are many more ways out there to make money than these five, but they give you a starting place and offer step-by-step instructions on how to get started.

You will find:

- How to make money through investing
- Making money through Amazon
- Becoming an online life coach
- Making money through affiliate marketing
- And much more

This book will also help you to realize if making money online is for you or not, as well as making sure you understand the pros and cons. It's not going to be easy or simple, but it can be done if you go into it with the right mentality.

www.ingramcontent.com/pod-product-compliance
Lightning Source LLC
Chambersburg PA
CBHW050022230526
45470CB00003B/1085